Love Rhythm

Apostle Andrea Lewis

Selah Communications, Inc.

All Scriptures are from the KJV.

Selah Communications, Inc.
PO Box 79493
Atlanta, GA 30357

Library of Congress Control Number: 2016907061

ISBN: 978-0-9909449-9-7 (Hardcover)

10 9 8 7 6 5 4 3 2 1

Dedication

To my Mother who is Love that bore me, and my Father who is Jesus that raised me up to love so powerfully as I do.

[O that thou wert as my brother, that sucked the breasts of my mother! When I should find thee without, I would kiss thee; yea, I should not be despised.
I would lead thee, and bring thee into my mother's house, who would instruct me: I would cause thee to drink of spiced wine of the juice of my pomegranate.
His left hand should be under my head, and his right hand should embrace me.
I charge you, O daughters of Jerusalem, that ye stir not up, nor awake my love, until he please.
Who is this that cometh up from the wilderness, leaning upon her beloved? I raised thee up under the apple tree: there thy mother brought thee forth: there she brought thee forth that bare thee.

Set me as a seal upon thine heart, as a seal upon thine arm: for love is strong as death; jealousy is cruel as the grave: the coals thereof are coals of fire, which hath a most vehement flame.

Many waters cannot quench love, neither can the floods drown it: if a man would give all the substance of his house for love, it would utterly be contemned.

We have a little sister, and she hath no breasts: what shall we do for our sister in the day when she shall be spoken for?

If she be a wall, we will build upon her a palace of silver; and if she be a door, we will inclose her with boards of cedar.

I am a wall, and my breasts like towers: then was I in his eyes as one that found favour.

Solomon had a vineyard at Baalhamon; he let out the vineyard unto keepers; every one for the fruit thereof was to bring a thousand pieces of silver.

My vineyard, which is mine, is before me: thou, O Solomon, must have a thousand, and those that keep the fruit thereof two hundred.

Thou that dwellest in the gardens, the companions hearken to thy voice: cause me to hear it.

Make haste, my beloved, and be thou like to a roe or to a young hart upon the mountains of spices.
(Song of Solomon 8:1-14)]

Table of Contents

Acknowledgments

Sweet to my taste
Wonderful to my touch
Easy to behold with eyes of love
Eternal love
Tenderhearted, so easily bruised
Never again alone and naked
Ecstasy, entranced
Seduce me with your eyes
Sexy, from head to toe, every inch, every facet of you

This is for you babe, and inspired by you.
Don't wake me I'm dreaming.

"THE GEM" You are as a pearl still in its shell and as a diamond in the rough. Though you are still covered as a pearl within the walls of its shell and still have dust of coal as a diamond uncut and unpolished, I see you and I know your true value and beauty. You have endured much but here you stand in strength and beauty. You are treasured.

I am sorry for every pain you ever felt in your life.
Please let my love heal you, you will never regret it.
Our love is natural, real, true, undeniable, blessed, our hearts are one.
Let us both breathe in our love;
we are not two in our love but three forevermore.
I am ready, truly ready and unashamed,
be with me Sweetness.

You know our love was meant to be. On T'aime
One Love (a love without impurities between chosen mates joined to God).

Ma douceur, je t'aime pour la vie.
(Sweetness, I love you eternally.)

Je tout suis, mon amour, dire oui, plaire.

8

Foreword

Cast me not away for I have heeded unto you; you are pleasantness to my soul.

Love, who can escape it, who can handle it: no one; just let it flow through you, just let it work.
Just let love work.

Love is as water, sometimes tumultuous, still the beauty and power of it is captivating. Tend to your love and prevent any erosion at the structure and foundation of it.

Even in its peaceful serene state, love, like water, must be tended to or it will become stagnant and undesirable. Always tend to your love, making sure nothing unpleasant is growing on the bottom that will alter its beauty.

Love Rhythm

This poem speaks Wisdom about the love of God placed in me, extended to the one (ones) my heart feels it for, given freely.

Eternal Love

A Love that never ceases and changes not is the Love to behold and feel,
let it heal you then give as you have received,
be not as those who are given to change.

I feel my heart physically breaking inside my chest, there is a piercing horrible pain bursting out from my heart, I have to let this love go. My heart reached out to God to take this love away but He sees the end that it is good. This poem speaks simple truth to steady the heart.

Love & Pain

Is Love worth the pain?
OR,
Is pain worth the Love?
Answer: YES.

Passion burned in me. Doesn't God surely speak to every emotion the heart carries? It is all good, all pure, all sweet, all awesome. I am in Love, praise God! So, sealed with a kiss, this poem speaks.

Red

Red is the color of my love for you coursing through my veins.
Red is the color of my blush when you smile at me.
Red is the color of a rose so beautiful, so soft, so fierce as you.
Red is the color of my eyes should you ever make me cry by leaving.
Red is the color of your lips so kissable so sweet.
Red, Red, my baby, my love, Red, yeah! Red.

I was thinking how beautiful my lover was and the facets of our relationship and God sent these words flowing through my mind. At this stage of our relationship our love was a beautiful and painful experience.

My Rose

Oh! The scent of you...
Your nectar is sweet to my taste.
So pleasant, so lovely to behold, let me look closely at you my love.
So many different colors, as your moods and ways with me
Red - a passionate lover of all that is me, entirely
Pink - are you as enamored by me as I see
Yellow - a constant friend, my best friend
White - so pure and real with me, always
Black - we will never again see that, I forgive you
Mauve - these are the times you are as a stranger to me, so different,
patience and understanding are needed.
I can never go, your uniqueness makes me desire you more; more to un-
derstand, more to learn, I am willing.
Many are your colors; many are your moods and ways with me
Your petals - as your soft velvety smooth skin, tantalizing me with ev-
ery touch
Yet you are so delicate, when touched roughly by words or lack of care

you are so easily bruised and broken with pain.
As the morning dew your sweat glistens on your moist body, it calls to me,
I'm in awe of your beauty.
Your stem - as the core of you, so tall, so strong, so fierce, holds together everything that is you in strength.
Your pricks - covering/guarding the core of you from being touched and held and handled,
Oh! So dangerous, Oh! How they made me bleed every time I reached out and touched you, because I was so inexperienced never yet having such gorgeous yet complicated one as you.
Many and random are the pricks that cover you. One careless or ignorant move I make with you and you cause me to hurt so much. Don't touch, don't come close "Don't love me" you say, while you are dying to be loved and held, who understands this but me?
One by one I removed your pricks with my love and gentleness, now I am safe with you and you are safe with me, to touch and embrace and caress you.
Your leaves - as your two arms, raised and open and reaching out as if to embrace me,
Oh! How I long to run into them.
My wonderful precious rose, my love, I have learned, I know you so well.
Let me nurture you, you will forever blossom in these hands of mine.

Lovely you are, and lovely you will remain in my care, always.
You have awakened ALL my senses and more.
In a garden of roses and flowers alike, there is none as you, my special rose.
You are a love flower, made to be loved and to cause a love of you in others,
Oh! How I adore you, ALL of you.

I had a need to wrap myself in our love, my heart was pleading that my lover look past all that would cause hesitation straight into the heart of God and join me in this unending love. So, these words flowed through me.

Forever

Please come with me...
Forever looking into your gorgeous eyes
Forever holding your hand
When you lean against me you cause a stir in me, a stir of excitement &
pleasure & comfort & belonging, Forever.
Forever hearing you laugh, Forever seeing you smile,
Forever Beautiful, Forever Sweetness, Forever Love,
Forever family, Forever mine, Forever yours,
Forever holding you, Forever being in your arms.
Full body massages, drawn baths, roses, petals, feeding you sweet treats,
one lover pleasing the other, heart-mind-body - completely, Forever.
Forever Christmases, Forever Thanksgivings,
Forever birthdays, Forever Holidays, Forever Valentine,
Forever vacations, Forever anniversaries,
Forever sweet kisses, Forever love-talks, Forever my baby,
Forever joy, Forever truth, Forever faithful, Forever together,
Forever dreams fulfilled, Forever passions satisfied,

25

Forever ONE heart-mind-kindred spirits,
Forever real, Forever right, Forever good to you,
Forever, not as people say but as God - Eternal,
Forever nurturing you,
Come on Sweetness take my hand; don't be afraid, God knows the way.
Are you ready babe, let's go.... FOREVER!!

Has anyone ever had a need? There was an overwhelming feeling in me; I was in need of my lover. Will God permanently fill this need for me? My heart waits, and my soul speaks.

I Need You There

I need you there to share my joy. I need you there to share my sorrow.
I need you there to hold my hand. I need you there to kiss my lips.
I need you there to make love to me. I need you there to speak love to me.
I need you there to wrap me in your arms. I need you there finding comfort in my arms.
I need you there to smile that smile that melts my heart. I need you there to laugh that laugh that thrills me.
I need you there to love me unconditionally as I love you. I need you there to make me laugh as you do.
I need you there to be tender the way you are.
I need you there to focus on our love, not things of pride or what people say.
I need you there to receive all of me, I am completely yours.
I need you there to give me all of you, trust me.
I need you there strong as you are. I need you there to fight for us, it is worth it.

29

I need you there to always be my Sweetness. I need you there always. I need you there to need me. I need you, Sweetness, please be there. Many have said always and forever, you know I live what I say. When you need me just look right beside you, I am there, always and forever.

My motivation is Sweetness, my first TRUE love.

The ability to express heart and soul emotion is a gift given and used by God through me, for God is love, true love, and all aspects of love.

The one your heart reaches for may question but let love speak.

This poem "Infatuation Or Love" arrived because although infatuation resembles love there is proof of the certainty of love and a permanency to love, true love, that will be evident to eyes that see and hearts that feel.

Thank you for the gift of love, sweet Jesus, my Master, my Guide, my Friend.

Infatuation Or Love

Infatuation - fleeting false thoughts of forever bordering on lust & obsession,
OR
Love - truth, eternal, passion, infinite undying soul connection.

Infatuation - I want you, feels at times like I need you, but I can live without you,
OR
Love - I have an eternal need of you.

Infatuation - when will someone I like more come along and what thing will make me say I had enough; I wonder if you're the one, it would be nice if you were,
OR
Love - no one and nothing will change me from you; unconditional; you are my perfect love.

Infatuation - so many things and ones turn my head,
OR
Love - am I able to stray; I see you in others always and none compare.

I have visited infatuation with others but I live in love with you. I am home!!

You please me very much, our love has engulfed me eternally; all my senses are active when you are near me.

The scent you wear arouses me and fills me with longing for you

My eyes love to behold you, none compare; my sight is fixed on you

I love what I feel, so soft and smooth and warm; very tantalizing

I want to hear you forever; your laugh, your voice, your love sounds

Oh! the taste of you, is there anything better to me, no; you are my love fruit, completely

I am aware of your essence, you satisfy me; my hunger is filled when in your presence

Are you aware of what you do to me? Even in the storm you will never lose me, I am yours forever. I love you.

What You Do To Me

I think of walks in the park and along the beach
I think of holding hands and being arm in arm giving tender delicious kisses one to another
I think of beautiful sunsets and long drives with you, I look at you and you take my breath away
I think of comfort days and nights, snuggled together whispering sweet things of love
I think of foot and body massages only for your pleasure, feeding you delectable things
I think of starry and moon lit nights as we gaze above, romantic trips and picnics
I think of us watching our children grow and prosper, I promised God to never leave you
I think of you on our day and that awesome ring on your finger, we belong
I want us to talk for hours about us as we touch and caress and stroke each other

37

I want us to play and laugh and have fun and tease and flirt always, I adore you
I want to give you all you desire of this world on a gold and platinum platter
You perplex me with your ways and moods but I am willing to learn, you are worth it
I hope in the day you will trust me with your whole self, I am your other half
I wonder when we will know each other as God intends, stand by my side all the rest of your years
I believe we will grow very old together without our love fading; it's as a river that runs strong and deep
I believe our family will look to us as their compass for love, it's unconditional and complete
I know our spirits yearn to be connected and God waits to be one with us
I see the day you will believe as I believe and know as I know, nothing will separate us
I see your smile and hear your laughter, it resounds in my spirit
I see all our dreams coming to full fruition as God so desires them
You are an embodiment of love to me, I accept everything about you
This and more is what you do to me, and I thank God for you.

Playful words though true for my Love who is so fun and wonderful and has me engulfed in emotion, enraptured.

Hooked

I'm hooked on you.
Your eyes, your hair, your lips;
Are you hooked on me too?
I want you hooked on me.
Study me, my curves, my perfume, my essence,
Remember the way I touch you, remember my taste,
Breathe me, can you feel me, Yeah, just like that!
Are you satisfied? Are you hooked yet? I am.

Words to question the things and behaviors I saw, and why my Love was so with me

Love/Hate

Am I creeping or am I just living.
Why do you fear me if you love me.
Why does my shadow or footsteps make you want to run and hide.
Do you love me or do you hate me.
Why do you smile at me one minute, and the next you can't look at me.
Why do you make plans as if to hold me forever, then send me away as
if there's no hope for us.
Am I loving you as I need to or am I hurting you.
Do I remind you of a past mistake or pain.
Do you see ME or do I reflect someone else.
Will you let me love you forever and make you feel safe.
Do you love me or do you hate me.
Will you let my love heal your pain, don't turn away.
Do you love me or do you hate me.
You hate it when I don't look at you.
You hate it when I don't speak.
You can't let me go can you.

Do you love me.
Do you hate me.
Let me reflect.
Do you hate me, I hate the games.
Do you love me...
I love you, too.

My soul cried out in a moment of loneliness with a heart needing to feel secure and connected. This is a poetic song my soul sang to comfort itself, but comfort was not found.

46

Don't Ask

If you loved me I need not ask.
If you wanted me I need not wonder.
If you knew me to be THE one I need not be lonely.
If you trusted me it would show.
If you believed, you could not turn nor walk away.
If you yearned for me you would not send me away.
If your world were not fine without me you would be here.
If your dreams included me there would be help.
If you needed me you would never lose me.
Do I love you? Don't ask, you need not.

Move On (Prelude)

Are you gone or are you just afraid.
I am still here, I am lonely and afraid.
We will work, you know.
Infatuation moves on, lust moves on,
all things not real moves on,
but love waits...

Move On

I can move on from the looks that make me feel dirty.
I can move on from the words that pierce as a sword.
I can move on from the way you control.
I can move on from the lies.
I can move on from the games.
I can move on from the harsh coldness.
BUT...
How do I move on from the looks that make me melt?
How do I move on from the words so sweet to my soul?
How do I move on from the way you give yourself to me?
How do I move on from the truth that escapes your lips?
How do I move on from the games of love we play?
(You know just what captures me; we see eye to eye.)
How do I move on from the warmth and tenderness YOU give?

...

What makes you so cold & bitter? / What makes you so damn warm & sweet?

What makes you push me away? / What makes you draw me close?
Is the pain too much for me to bear? / Is the love too much for me to handle?
MOVE ON!!!
I can move on from the pain, but how do I move on from the love.
"I love her so much I just want to be with her." How do I move on from that!!!
TRUE LOVE, true love, TRUE LOVE... I can't move on!!!

True love is a glorious thing but we don't always know how to handle it and we cannot, only God can because He is the author of it and love is God Himself. He allows us to feel it and guides us in it. We don't know the ins and outs of it, and its multitude of emotions will overwhelm us if we don't let God work (let love work). He will get us in sync with the one His given love has joined us to. In sync, love gives a flood of good emotions - ride the waves. Out of sync we develop a flood of wrong emotions that tear us as the waves crash in on us but He sees our heart and understands so He gives us His finger to hold on to and pulls us to shore to WAIT for the next good wave. Don't become afraid, BE ATTENTIVE and ride it well, God is there, God is with you, His love is in you, true love has purpose and will not fail. What have we learned: patience, trust, be attentive, and SUBMIT to love, you will be riding the waves by at the very least 90% the other 10% won't kill you if you hold on to God. I rest in this truth.

What You Do To Me (You Move Me)

You move me to pain
You move me to joy
You move me to ecstasy
You move me to sorrow
I wear my heart on my sleeve
Oh what you do to me
You move me to laughter
You move me to agony
You move me to passion
You move me to fear
You excite me
What you do to me my love
You move me to romance
You move me to want to leave
You move me to stay
You move me to trust
I want more of you, please.

What you do to me Sweetness
You move me to love
You move me to forever
You move me to completeness
You move me to say yes
Our love is in God and God in us
What you do to me, only you.

I would always look at my love and knew I was looking at beauty but one evening I was looking at this beautiful face in a picture on my computer screen and my heart was full so I began to magnify different portions of the picture and all I could say repeatedly is "Oh! My God, Wow, Wow" There was NO imperfection or impurities in ANY strength magnification. I beheld perfect beauty, save God. I had a very real conversation with God and thanked Him.
The words flowed from this enlightened experience.

Beautiful

I think of you always. I am captured by your beauty.
I gaze at your eyes and I am lost in them.
I look at your nose so perfectly formed and I am amazed.
I stare at your lips unendingly, they call to me; they are the shape of love.
Your skin is so flawless and radiant I am in awe that God made one as you.
Your face my love gives me great appreciation for the work of God's hands and Has my heart searching for words it fails to find to understand how perfect beauty stands before me and that I would dare to call you mine.
I have been truly blessed; Oh! Most beautiful one.

Find me always by your side
All that I am, I am yours; we belong
I love you so very much, eternally with precision
Trust me to always catch you from falling
Hold on
Full of the love God planted and raised in me for you
Unconditional
Love waits
LOVE
You are in my soul, connected, one, He holds you there.

May I (My Angel Eyes)

May I touch the part of you that is emphatically real and true
May I hold your hand so soft and strong
May I kiss your lips so perfectly formed
May I keep your heart, I treasure your love
May I caress your cheek, oh most handsome
May I stroke you in comfort; we are in a good place
May I ease your pain; too much pain
May I catch you from falling; always on time
May I stay forever; "I ain't goin' no-where!"
May I cover you with my love, this is certain
May I feel your embrace, oh how I need your arms
May I gaze into your angel eyes; in them our love is complete
May I as long as I breathe love you, for I do, so much!

Post-word

The love in me is perfect, but, I am still a work in progress.
I love you babe.

Encouragement

An Apostle of Jesus Christ by the will of God, to the saints, and to the faithful in Christ Jesus.
Ephesians 1.

The cry: Lord please speak to Your children. Comfort all the hearts that You have guided to love.

The answer: O Lord God of hosts, who is a strong Lord like unto Thee? or to Thy faithfulness round about Thee? Psalm 89:8

"Have you ever had a love?"

"You give me Butterflies."
"I love her so much, I just want to be with her."

OneLove

The beginning and the end is love.

Amen (Truly, so be it).

www.ingramcontent.com/pod-product-compliance
Lightning Source LLC
Chambersburg PA
CBHW042011090426
42811CB00015B/1613